S IS FOR SLUGGER

THE ULTIMATE BASEBALL ALPHABET

"BIG PAPI"
DAVID ORTIZ

BY **JAMES LITTLEJOHN**   ILLUSTRATED BY **MATTHEW SHIPLEY**

ROBERTO CLEMENTE

To Dad, for taking me to see Rickey, Terry,
Carney, Eck, and more. — J.L.

To Mom and Dad, and ice cream
in little plastic baseball caps. — M.S.

Library of Congress Cataloging-in-Publication Data available upon request.

This book is available in quantity at special discounts for your group or organization. For further information, contact:
Triumph Books LLC, 814 North Franklin Street, Chicago, Illinois 60610
(312) 337-0747
www.triumphbooks.com

Printed in USA
ISBN: 978-1-62937-796-4

A IS FOR ACE

Always accurate, 4-time Cy Young winner Greg Maddux
spent 23 seasons straight dealing.

DENNIS ECKERSLEY

ROLLIE FINGERS

B IS FOR BULLPEN

Call for help! If the starter struggles,
you gotta turn to the 'pen.

C IS FOR CAPTAIN CLUTCH

Respect. New York legend Derek Jeter came through when it counted and led his club to 5 championships.

THE PHILLIE PHANATIC

BO JACKSON

"BIG MAC"
MARK McGWIRE

MIKE PIAZZA

"THE ROCKET"
ROGER CLEMENS

"MR. PADRE"
TONY GWYNN

D IS FOR DUGOUT

Waiting their turn or ready in a pinch, there are colorful characters up and down the bench.

"CRIME DOG"
FRED McGRIFF

KENNY LOFTON

"THE KILLER BEES"
CRAIG BIGGIO   JEFF BAGWELL

E IS FOR EXPRESS

5,714 strikeouts. 7 no-hitters. 4 decades.
"The Ryan Express" powered through hitters like a freight train.

NOLAN RYAN

F IS FOR FLAMETHROWER

He's on fire! Justin Verlander's flamin' hot fastballs can clock in at over 100 miles per hour.

G IS FOR GREEN MONSTER

It's no ordinary wall. Boston's big, bad Green Monster is known to eat up homers.

TED WILLIAMS

MANNY RAMÍREZ

BOS

AT BAT

H IS FOR HAMMERIN'

Bang! Bang! Boom! Hall of Famer "Hammerin'", Hank Aaron pounded a record-breaking 755 home runs.

I IS FOR IRON MAN

Taking consistency to another level, "The Iron Man" Cal Ripkin Jr. didn't miss a game for 17 years.

LOU GEHRI

KEN GRIFFEY JR.

J IS FOR JUNIOR

Smooth swinging, sweet fielding.
Fans couldn't take their eyes off "The Kid."

KKKKKKKKKKKKKKKKeout

Steeeeee-rike 3! The letter K holds a special place in every pitcher's heart.

SANDY KOUFAX

L IS FOR LASER

Some baserunners learn too late,
but everyone knows: Never run on Ichiro.

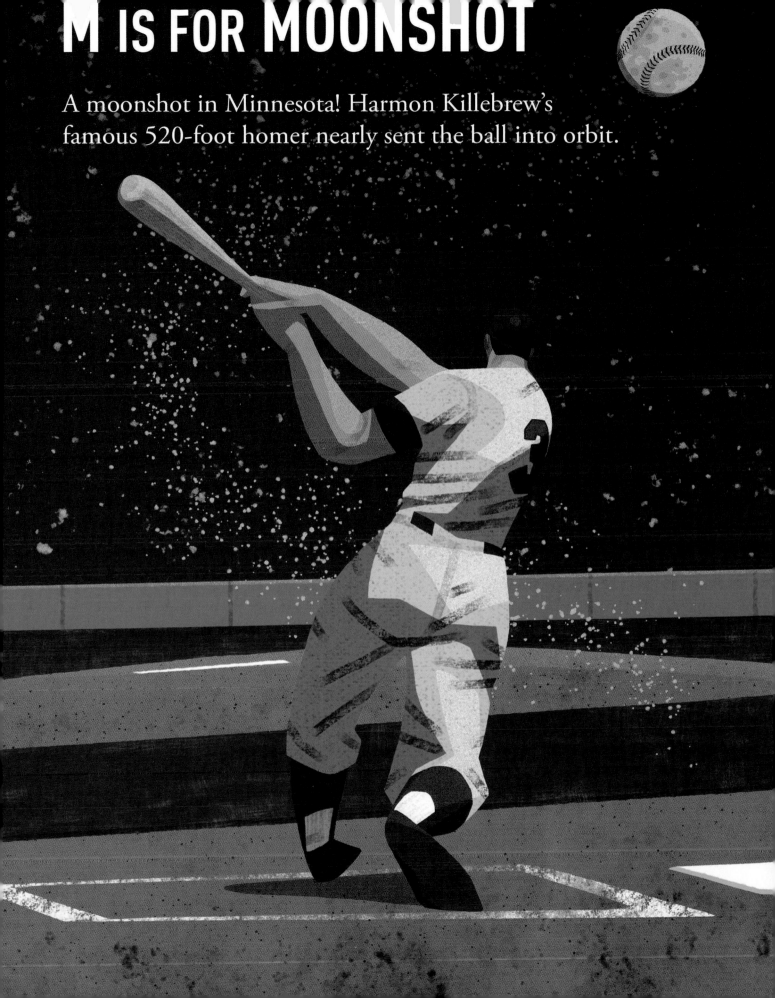

M IS FOR MOONSHOT

A moonshot in Minnesota! Harmon Killebrew's famous 520-foot homer nearly sent the ball into orbit.

N IS FOR NO-NO

How many no-no's could a Nomo throw
if a Nomo could throw no mo' no-no's?

HIDEO "THE TORNADO" NOMO

O IS FOR OCTOBER

As the autumn leaves fall, the games matter more. Saving his best for the playoffs turned Reggie Jackson into "Mr. October."

P IS FOR PIONEERS

It takes courage to go first. In '47, Jackie Robinson did just that, making history as the first African American to play in the majors.

In '53, Mamie "Peanut" Johnson became the first woman to pitch in the Negro Leagues. Just 5-foot-3, she stood tall with a 33-8 record over three trailblazing seasons.

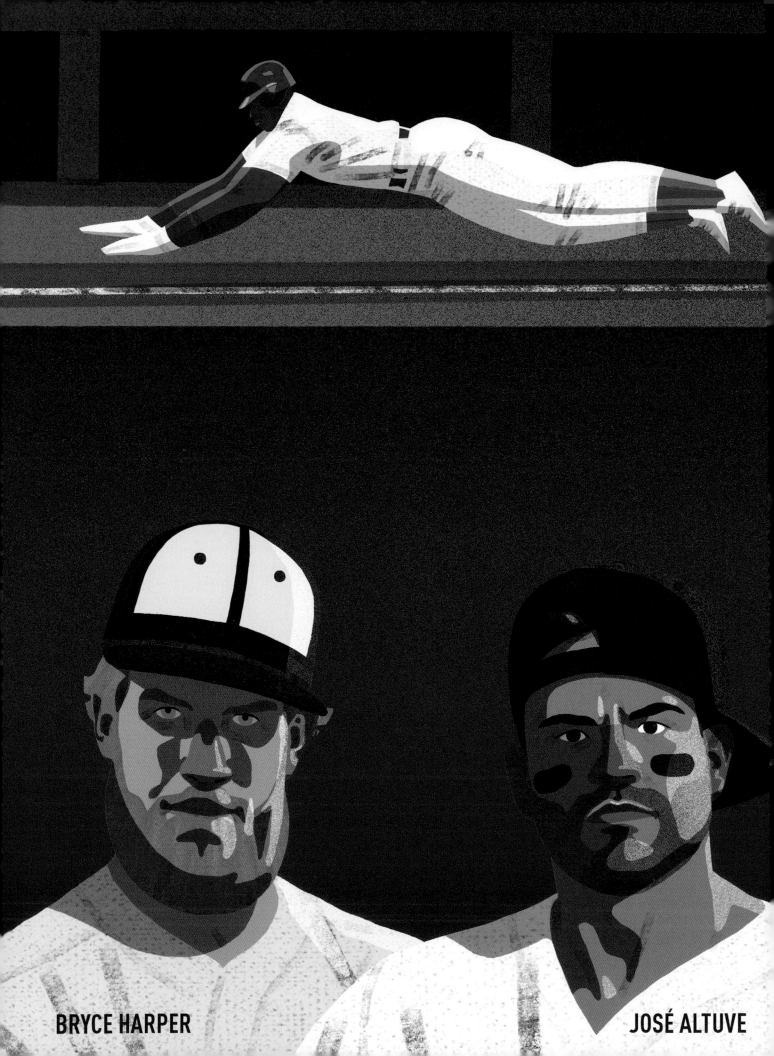

BRYCE HARPER

JOSÉ ALTUVE

Q IS FOR QUICK

Run, Rickey, run! The super-speedy Rickey Henderson stole 1,406 bases — no one else has even swiped 1,000.

R IS FOR RALLY CAP

The difference between winning and losing can come down to one thing: A willingness to wear your hat inside out.

CHRISTIAN YELICH   KRIS BRYANT

S IS FOR SULTAN OF SWAT

The Sultan of Swat. The King of Crash. The Colossus of Clout.
The Titan of Terror. The Great Bambino. BABE. RUTH.

T IS FOR TROUT

The rarest and most valuable of all fish, the *angel trout* is known to play center field and crush baseballs.

MIKE TROUT

U IS FOR BIG UNIT

Watch out! Towering almost
7 feet tall, Randy Johnson
stands as one of the most
intimidating pitchers
of all time.

V IS FOR VACUUM

Good luck getting one past him. Brooks
"The Human Vacuum Cleaner" Robinson
sucked up 16 straight Gold Gloves at third base.

W IS FOR WIZARD

Ozzie Smith – the flipping, flying "Wizard of Oz" – redefined what a shortstop could do.

X IS FOR SOX

Who needs cleats? White Sox legend "Shoeless" Joe Jackson once played a game in his stockings…and the nickname stuck.

BARRY BONDS

Y IS FOR GOIN' YARD

He hits it high…he hits it deep…it is outta here!!!

Z IS FOR ZZZZZZZZZZZZZZZZZZs

Once the Sandman enters, it's time for bed. Closer
Mariano Rivera put bats to sleep with a record 652 saves.